Collins

INTERNATIONAL PRIMARY ENGLISH AS A SECOND LANGUAGE

Workbook 1

An imprint of HarperCollins*Publishers*
The News Building
1 London Bridge Street
London SE1 9GF

browse the complete Collins catalogue at
www.collins.co.uk

Publisher Celia Wigley
Commissioning editor Karen Jamieson
Series editor Karen Morrison
Managing editor Sarah Thomas
Editor Alexander Rutherford
Project managed by Tara Alner
Edited by Tracy Thomas
Proofread by Zoe Smith
Cover design by ink-tank and associates
Cover artwork by Milly Teggle
Typesetting by QBS Learning
Illustrations by QBS Learning and Beehive Illustration Agency
Production by Lauren Crisp

Printed and bound by Grafica Veneta S. P. A.

All exam-style questions and sample answers have been written by the author. In examinations marks may be given differently.

Text acknowledgements
The publishers gratefully acknowledge the permissions granted to reproduce copyright material in the book. Every effort has been made to contact the holders of copyright material, but if any have been inadvertently overlooked, the Publisher will be pleased to make the necessary arrangements at the first opportunity.

p88 poem The Ball Song by Tony Mitton from *Playtime Rhymes*, compiled by John Forster, published by Oxford University Press 1998, reprinted by permission of David Higham Associates.

Photo acknowledgements
The publishers wish to thank the following for permission to reproduce photographs. Every effort has been made to trace copyright holders and to obtain their permission for the use of copyright materials. The publishers will gladly receive any information enabling them to rectify any error or omission at the first opportunity.

(t = top, c = centre, b = bottom, r = right, l = left)

Cover & p1 Milly Teggle

HarperCollins*Publishers* Limited for: Artwork from *My Family Tree* by Zoe Clarke, illustrated by Anne Wilson, text © 2010 Zoe Clarke. Artwork from *Bad Bat* by Laura Hambleton, illustrated by Laura Hambleton, text © 2011 Laura Hambleton. Artwork from *What's for Breakfast?* by Paul Shipton, illustrated by Jon Stuart, text © 2006 Paul Shipton. Artwork from *Bob's Secret Hideaway* by Tom Dickinson, illustrated by Jimothy Oliver, text © 2014 Tom Dickinson. Artwork from Jack and the Beanstalk by Caryl Hart, illustrated by Nicola L. Robinson, text © 2013 Caryl Hart. Artwork from *The Oak Tree* by Anna Owen, illustrated by Laszlo Veres, text © 2005 Anna Owen. Artwork from *Bones* by Jonathan Emmett and Alan Baker, artwork by Steve Lumb, text © 2010 Jonathan Emmett and Alan Baker. Artwork from *Sam the Big, Bad Cat* by Sheila Bird, illustrated by Trish Phillips, text © 2005 Sheila Bird. Artwork from *A Day Out* by Anna Owen, illustrated by Andy Hammond, text © 2005 Anna Owen.

P62t Kencana Studio/Ss, p62c Omer N Raja/Ss, p62b Solphoto/Ss, p72a Corepics VOF/Ss, p72b stephen rudolph/Ss, p72d Syda Productions/Ss p72e Stefan Holm/Ss, p72f Margo Harrison/Ss, p72g Maciej Kopaniecki/Ss, p72h shinobi/Ss, p72i Bplanet/Ss, p72j 9comeback/Ss, p82h Ruslan Kudrin/Ss, p82i Karina Bakalyan/Ss, p82j Roman Sigaev/Ss, p101l Skreidzeleu/Ss, p101r Alamy/dbimages, p104l Getty Images/Digital Vision/Lottie Davies, p104c Skreidzeleu/Ss, p104r Alamy/Andy Hockridge, p113a f9photos/Ss, p113b Eky Studio/Ss, p113c TravelMediaProductions/Ss, p113d Bon Appetit/Ss, p117 Pyty/Ss, p119tr ghrzuzudu/Ss, p119br, p151 Sergey Uryadnikov/Ss

Contents

Topic 1 Our school

Unit A What's your name?

1 Colour all the letters in your name.

Write your name.

_____

Use proper names.

2 **Draw a picture of yourself. Write your name.**

My name is _____.

My name begins with _____.

3 Write *his* or *her* under each picture.

a)

____her____ ball

b)

_____ book

c)

_____ laptop

d)

_____ cap

e)

_____ bag

f)

_____ lunch box

Use possessive adjectives.

4 **Draw a picture of your friend. Trace and complete the sentence.**

This is _____ .

Unit B In my classroom

1 Listen and write the first letter of each word.

chair	door	paper	scissors
computer	eraser	pencil	table
crayon	glue	ruler	whiteboard

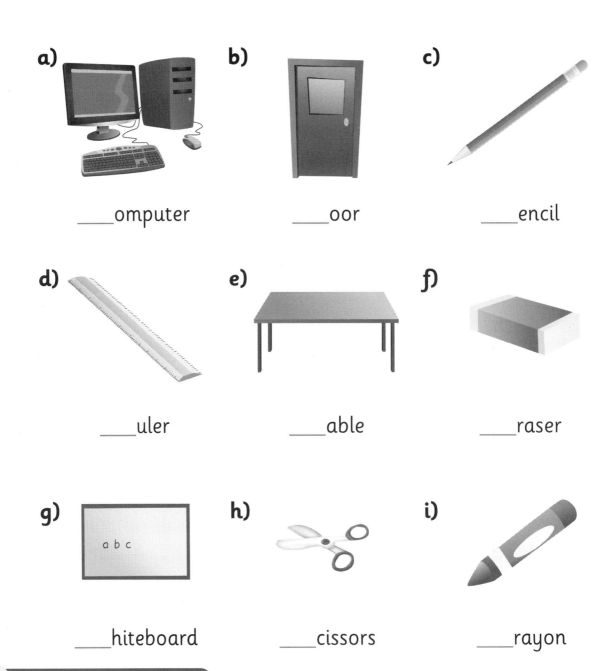

a) ____omputer

b) ____oor

c) ____encil

d) ____uler

e) ____able

f) ____raser

g) ____hiteboard

h) ____cissors

i) ____rayon

2 **Choose the correct word. Write the word under the picture.**

bin	pen	book	bag

a)

_____

b)

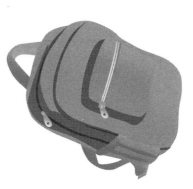

_____

c)

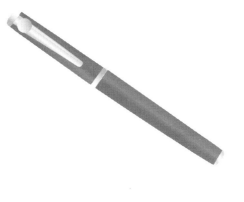

_____

d)

_____

3 **What letter does each word begin with?**
Circle the correct letter.

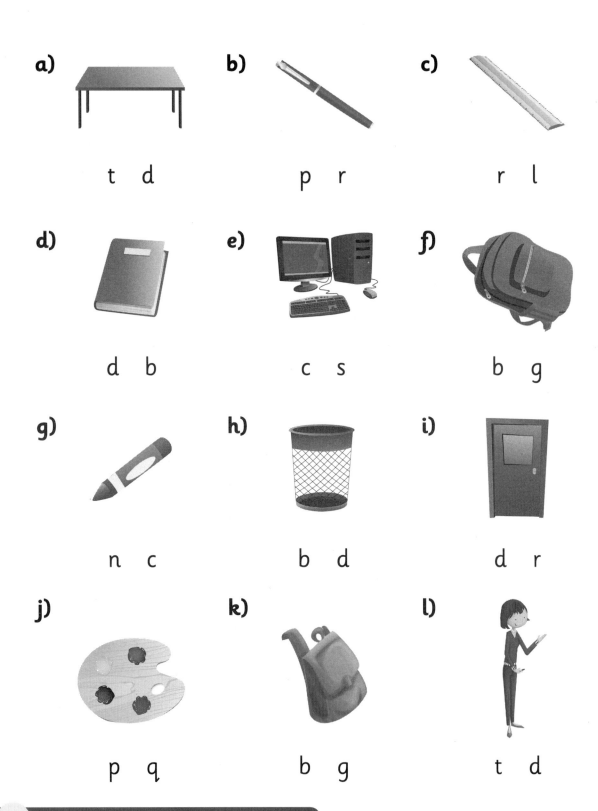

a)

t   d

b)

p   r

c)

r   l

d)

d   b

e)

c   s

f)

b   g

g)

n   c

h)

b   d

i)

d   r

j)

p   q

k)

b   g

l)

t   d

4 Find these words in the puzzle.

bag book crayon pen pencil ruler scissors table

t	c	p	e	n	c	i	l
a	n	k	l	y	u	n	t
b	a	g	m	v	c	y	p
l	m	y	b	o	o	k	e
e	v	c	r	a	y	o	n
t	c	x	y	p	o	m	t
r	u	l	e	r	c	y	x
s	c	i	s	s	o	r	s

5 Trace the words here. Say each word.

pen

bag

book

ruler

pencil

table

crayon

scissors

6 **Which path has the letters of the alphabet in the correct order? Where does this path take the girl?**

Recognise letters of alphabet.

Unit C What I do at school

1 **Match the words and the pictures. The first one has been done for you.**

a) run

b) read

c) skip

d) listen

e) jump

f) sing

g) write

h) play

2 What are they saying? Copy the correct sentence.

Listen.	Catch.
Sit down.	Open your book.

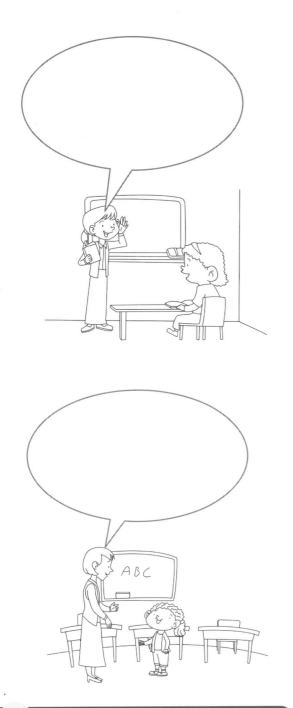

Understand imperative forms.

3 Complete the picture of the classroom. Show what is in your classroom. Talk about your picture.

Topic 1 **Progress check**

1 Listen and tick ✓ the pictures.

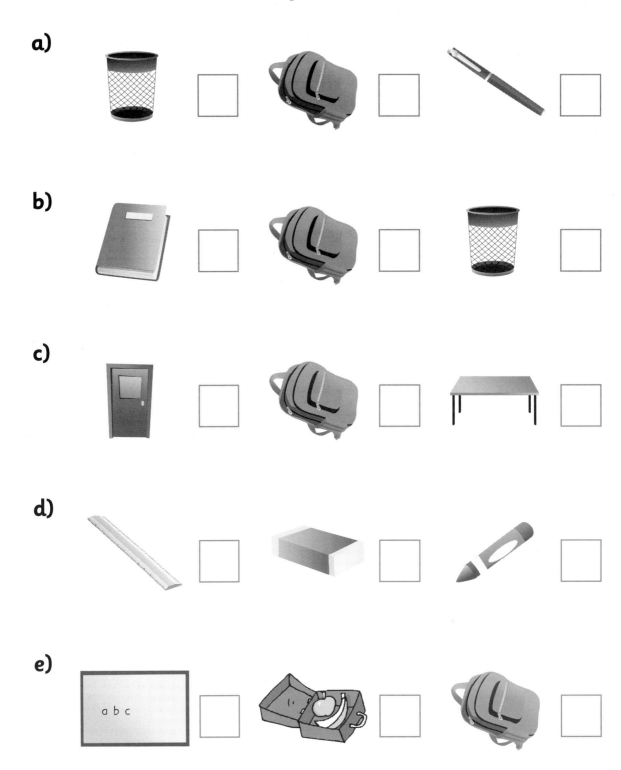

2 Listen and write the first letter.

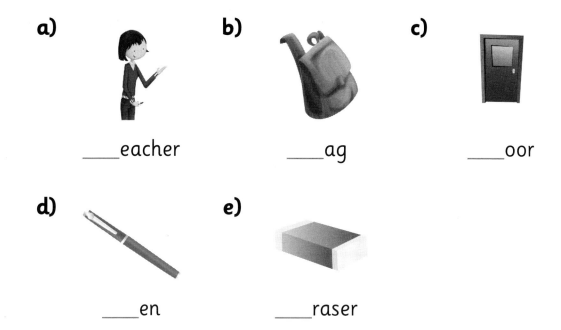

a) _____eacher

b) _____ag

c) _____oor

d) _____en

e) _____raser

3 Circle the two words that are the same in each box.

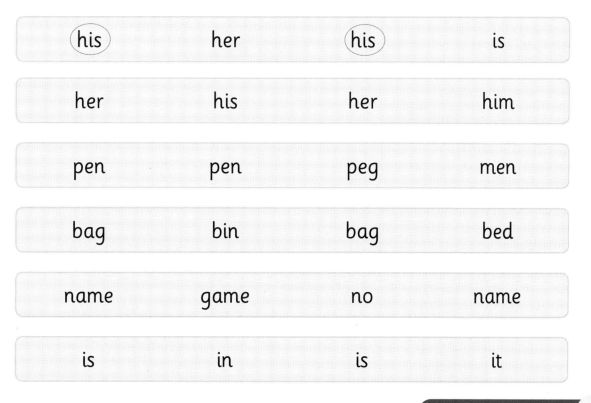

his	her	his	is
her	his	her	him
pen	pen	peg	men
bag	bin	bag	bed
name	game	no	name
is	in	is	it

Topic 2 All about me

Unit A All about me!

1 Tick ✓ the correct word.

a)

he ☐

she ☐

b)

they ☐

it ☐

c)

she ☐

it ☐

d)

I ☐

they ☐

Use personal subject pronouns.

2 **Circle the two words that are the same in each box.**

(I) you eye (I)

you yes you he

he she he her

she see she sea

it in it to

we will we when

they this they that

3 Complete the capital letters.

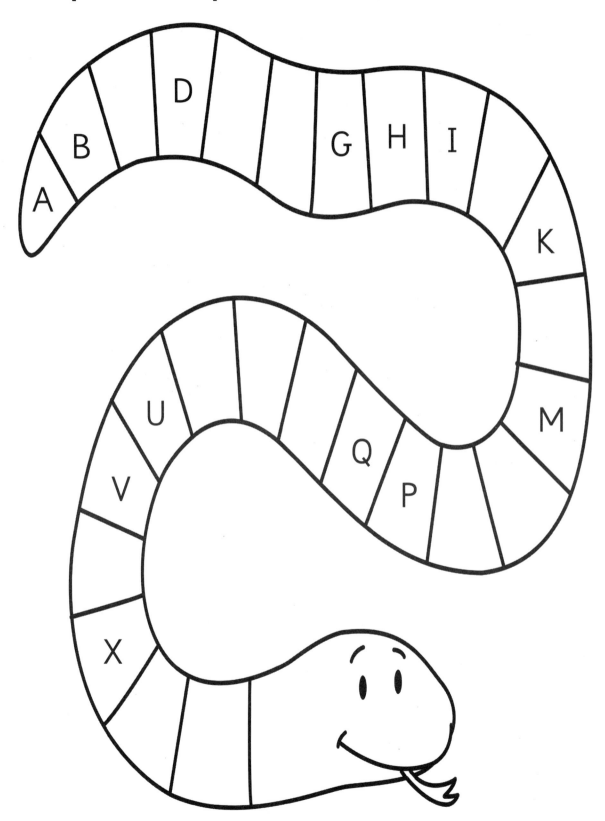

Recognise and write capital letters.

4 **Listen to your teacher. Complete each of these names with a capital letter from the box.**

| V | B | M | A | F | T | S | L | H |

a) ____ue

b) ____nton

c) ____oni

d) ____ary

e) ____ernando

f) ____usi

g) ____aile

h) ____ihaan

i) ____ucy

Write the names of three friends. Start with capital letters.

_____

_____

_____

5 Draw a picture of yourself, or glue in a photo.

6 Complete the sentences about yourself.

My name is _____.

I am _____ years old.

I am a _____.

Unit B My family

1 Circle all the words that begin with *b*.

brother   boy   dog   book

bag   girl   ball

2 Who are these people? Write the first two letters.

_____ _____ andma   _____ _____ andpa

3 Circle the words that end in –*er*.

Here   are   my   father   and   my   grandmother.

4 **Find eight family members in the word snake. Circle the words.**

5 **Draw a picture of your family. Label your picture.**

Use singular nouns.

6 Read the story *My Family Tree* in the Student's Book again.

- Complete the family tree.
- Use words from the box.

brother   Dad   grandparents   Mom   sister

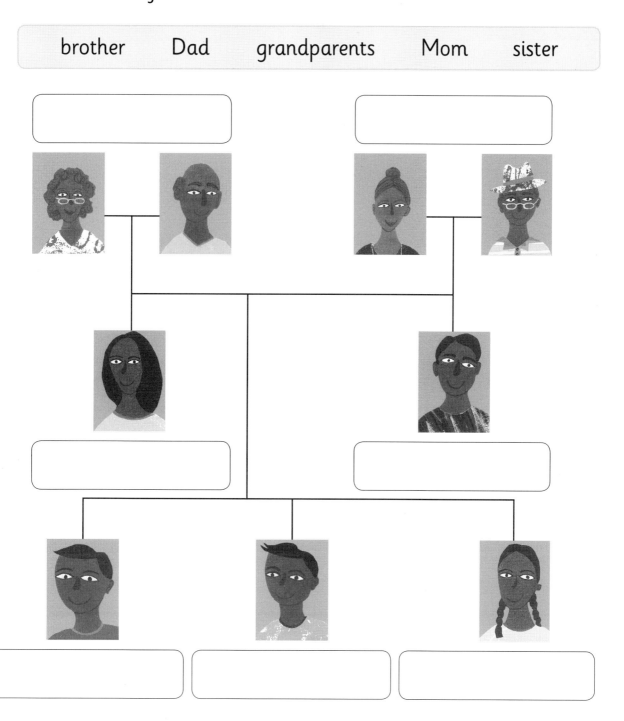

7 **Look at the first letter in each word. Write these words in alphabetical order.**

father sister brother mother grandma

_____

_____

_____

_____

8 **Write these family names in alphabetical order.**

Singh Lee Foster Ozawa Antwe

_____

_____

_____

_____

Use common and proper nouns.

9 Read this personal story about Jo.

My name is Jo. I am 7 years old.
This is my family.

This is my Mom. Her name is Nina.

I've got a big brother and sister.
My brother's name is Max and my
big sister's name is Lizzie.

This is my baby sister. Her name is
Sara. She is 1 year old.

I love my family!

10 Answer the questions.

a) Who is in Jo's family? Write their names.

_____Jo_____ _____ _____ _____ _____

b) How old is Jo? _____

c) How old is the baby? _____

d) Jo's mom is called _____.

Unit C What I do at home

1 Match the words and the pictures.

a)

drive

b)

eat

c)

cook

d)

wash

e)

sleep

f)

ride

2 **Look at the pictures. Circle the activities you can see. Say or write them.**

a)

b)

c)

d)

e)

f)

3 **Listen to the sentences. Circle all the words with the same 'a' sound as in** *cat*.

a) I have got a cat and a hat.

b) My gran has a nap in the afternoon.

c) I've got an apple in my hand.

d) Can you ride a bike? I can!

4 **Complete the words.**

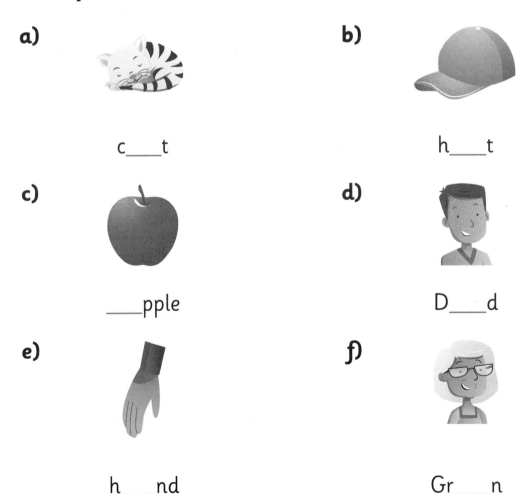

a) c___t

b) h___t

c) ___pple

d) D___d

e) h___nd

f) Gr___n

5 Write the correct word under each picture.

brush   cook   eat   hop   play   ride   run   sleep   wash

a)

_____

b)

_____

c)

_____

d)

_____

e)

_____

f)

_____

g)

_____

h)

_____

i)

_____

6 Read the story *Dad, Gran and the Cat Take a Nap* in the Student's Book. Complete the sentences with a word from the box.

cat   Dad   Gran   nap

a)

_____ needs a nap.

b)

_____ is on the sofa.

c)

The _____ is on the bench.

d)

Dad has a _____.

Use nouns and present simple verbs.

7 Complete the sentences. Choose words from the box.

can   can't   He   is

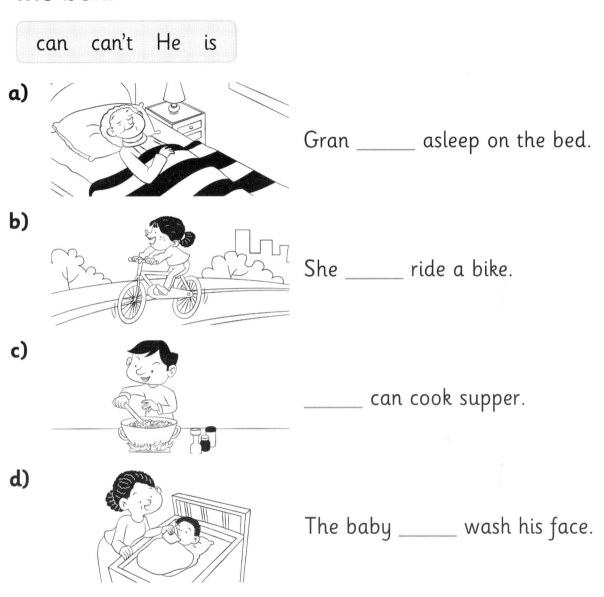

a) Gran _____ asleep on the bed.

b) She _____ ride a bike.

c) _____ can cook supper.

d) The baby _____ wash his face.

8 Complete these sentences about things you can and can't do.

a) I can _____.

b) I can't _____.

Topic 2 Progress check

1 Listen and tick ✓ the words.

a)

☐ he   ☐ it   ☐ she

☐ she   ☐ that   ☐ he

b)

☐ mother   ☐ grandpa   ☐ uncle

☐ father   ☐ grandma   ☐ aunty

2 Listen and tick ✓ the pictures.

a)

☐   ☐   ☐

b)

☐   ☐   ☐

3 **Complete the words.**

a)

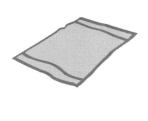

m____t

b)

h____nd

4 **Circle the correct word.**

a)

eat   sleep

b)

cook   book

c)

bike   bag

d)

wash   dish

Topic 3 Our colourful world

Unit A Colours

1 Listen and draw.

Use adjectives and colours.

2 Look at the pictures. Say the words. Write the beginning sounds.

a)

_____C_____

b)

_____

c)

_____

d)

_____

e)

_____

f)

_____

g)

_____

h)

_____

3 Colour in the colour words in the puzzle using the correct colour.

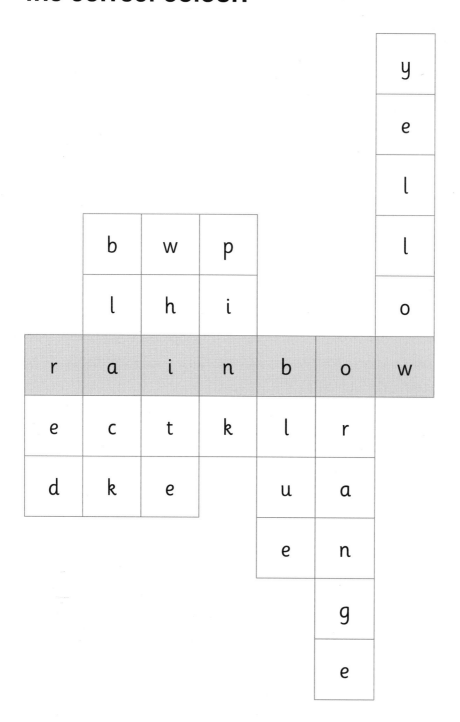

Read the word in the grey blocks.

4 **Choose four different things you can see in the classroom. Draw them and count how many you can see.**

Draw	How many?
1	
2	
3	
4	

5 **Listen to the poem _My Colouring Book_ again. Colour in the picture.**

6 **Add two people or two things to the picture. Colour them in.**

7 **Use a different colour to colour in these things. Write the name of the colour you use.**

A _____ pen.

A _____ notebook.

A _____ book.

A _____ pencil.

A _____ sharpener.

A _____ bag.

A _____ ruler.

A _____ pencil box.

Unit B Describing things

1 **Listen to the story *Rat-a-tat-tat*. Colour in the picture.**

2 **Use the words in the box to label the picture.**

| blue | cat | fox | hat | socks | white | yellow |

Use adjectives and colours and common nouns.

3 **Listen to the sentences. Then circle all the words with the 'o' sound like in the word *fox*.**

a) The dog and the frog are in the box.

b) The book is on the table.

4 **Listen to the sentences. Then circle all the words with the 'a' sound like in the word *cat*.**

a) The bad bat makes the mouse sad.

b) The bat makes the owl mad.

5 **Complete the words.**

a)

d ___ g

b)

fr ___ g

c)

b ___ t

d)

s ___ ck

e)

b ___ x

f)

f ___ x

6 Look at the pictures. What shapes can you see?

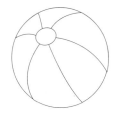   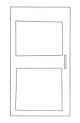

  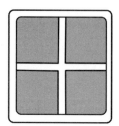 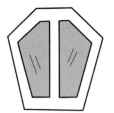

 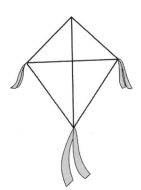

7 Count the shapes you can see in the pictures. Write your answers.

a) squares

b) circles

c) rectangles

_____   _____   _____

d) triangles

e) stars

f) hexagons

_____   _____   _____

Use numbers to count; use common nouns.

8 **Choose the correct sentences from the box.**

Copy the sentences next to the pictures.

Bat tricks Fox.	Owl is mad.
Bat tricks Mouse.	The dog is big.

a)

_____

_____

b)

_____

_____

c)

_____

_____

d)

_____

_____

Unit C How many?

1 Draw lines to match the numbers and the words.

1   seven

2   five

3   two

4   nine

5   one

6   six

7   four

8   eight

9   ten

10   three

2 Complete the game. Fill in the numbers.

- Play the game in pairs.
- Spin a spinner.
- Move your counters.
- Say the numbers.

3 Circle the correct words.

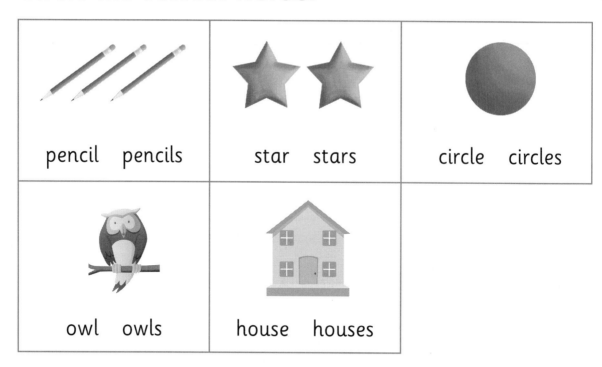

pencil   pencils

star   stars

circle   circles

owl   owls

house   houses

4 Tick ✓ the correct sentences.

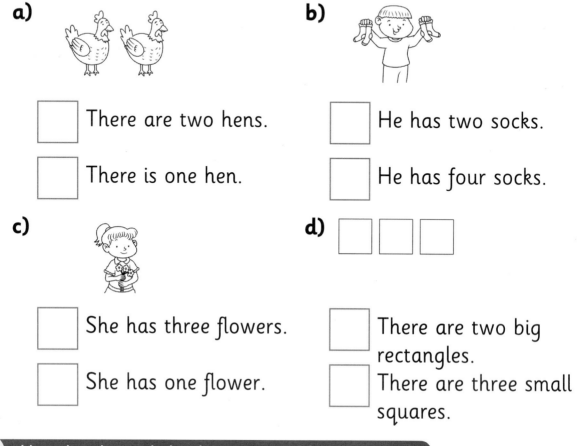

a)

☐ There are two hens.

☐ There is one hen.

b)

☐ He has two socks.

☐ He has four socks.

c)

☐ She has three flowers.

☐ She has one flower.

d)

☐ There are two big rectangles.

☐ There are three small squares.

Topic 3 Progress check

1 Listen and tick ✓ the words.

☐ yellow

☐ red

☐ blue

☐ orange

☐ green

☐ black

☐ white

☐ pink

☐ brown

☐ grey

☐ purple

2 Complete the words.

a)

b ___ t

b)

___ ___ x

c)

___ ___ x

d)

___ ___ g

3 Write the words that match the pictures.

> circle   eight   mouse   owl   rainbow
> six   square   triangle   two

a)

_____

b)

_____

c)

_____

d)

_____

e)

_____

f)

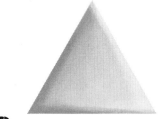

_____

g)

_____

h)

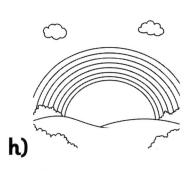

_____

i)

_____

Topic 4 Food

Unit A Fruit and vegetables

1 **Write the first letter of each word. Then draw your own picture.**

a)

_____pple

b)

_____range

c)

_____trawberry

d)

_____rapes

e)

_____elon

f)

_____ango

g)

_____umpkin

h)

_____arrot

2 **How many are there? Write the number words, then complete the words.**

a)

_____ carrot_____

b)

_____ fig_____

c)

_____ banana_____

d)

_____ melon_____

e)

_____ grape_____

f)

_____ orange_____

Use numbers to count; use common nouns.

3 Find the fruit and vegetable words in the word search puzzle.

apple   bean   cabbage   grape   guava

mango   onion   peach   potato   spinach

a	p	p	l	e	c	p	b	s
h	g	m	o	p	a	z	v	p
g	r	a	p	e	b	x	n	i
u	k	n	q	a	b	e	a	n
a	i	g	r	c	a	o	e	a
v	j	o	s	h	g	n	y	c
a	k	t	y	u	e	i	o	h
m	p	o	t	a	t	o	f	m
l	g	b	u	w	c	n	s	i

4 **Read the words. They are jumbled. Make them into sentences then write the sentences.**

a) two bananas There are.

_____

b) She tomatoes likes.

_____

c) apple This is round red a.

_____

d) you Do pineapples like?

_____

5 **Draw a picture of your favourite fruit or vegetable. Complete the sentence to go with your picture.**

I like _____ s.

6 Read the riddles. Draw pictures to show the answers.

a) I am long. I am orange and I am crunchy to eat. What am I?

b) I am small and round. I am green or red or yellow. I am soft and sweet. What am I?

c) I am big and round. I am orange or yellow. You cook me. What am I?

Unit B Let's eat

1 Complete the words.

a)

a h____t p____t

b)

s____x f____gs

c)

a b____g b____s

d)

t____n h____ns

e)

a f____t c____t

f)

s____n

2 How many 3-letter words can you make? Write them on the lines.

a) p a c d t m f o

_____

_____

b) l p o g t b n a i h

_____

_____

c) c u y m r e p n i f t

_____

_____

Recognise and sound phonemes.

3 Match the words and the times.

breakfast   tea   snack

dinner   lunch

4 What time do you have breakfast? Draw the hands on the clock.

5 Tick ✓ the correct sentence under each picture.

a)

☐ The ants like cake.

☐ The ants don't like cake.

b)

☐ The ants like apple.

☐ The ants don't like apple.

c)

☐ The ants like chocolate.

☐ The ants don't like chocolate.

d)

☐ Dad is sleeping.

☐ Dad is eating.

Use present simple verbs to give personal information.

6 **Answer the questions. Draw pictures.**
Describe your pictures to your group.

a) What do you like for breakfast? _____

b) What do you like for a snack? _____

c) What do you like for supper? _____

7 What are they doing? Circle the correct words.

a)

drinking   playing

b)

drawing   reading

c)

playing   eating

d)

jumping   playing

e)

writing   drinking

f)

singing   sleeping

8 **Draw things you need to make pancakes.**
Write the word underneath your picture.

eggs   flour   milk   sugar

Unit C **What I like**

1 Read *What do you like*? again. Answer the questions. Tick ✓ the answers.

a) What do you like for breakfast?

☐ eggs

☐ porridge

☐ toast

b) What does he like for a snack?

☐ yoghurt

☐ an apple

☐ cake

c) What does he like for lunch?

☐ a sandwich

☐ pizza

☐ baked potato

2 Circle the correct words.

a)

b)

c)

potato sandwich   cake cereal   biscuit banana

Use interrogatives and common nouns.

3 **Find things that Pedro likes in the word snake and circle them.**

4 **Make sentences. Put a full stop at the end of each sentence.**

a) I toast like and tea

_____

b) reading and playing She likes

_____

c) apples Grapes fruit are and

_____

d) for breakfast I cereal and milk like

_____

e) doesn't like Ali cheese fish and

_____

5 Look at the graph. Answer the questions.

What we like to drink

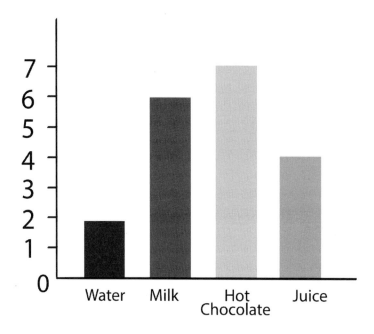

a) How many children like water?

_____

b) How many children like juice?

_____

c) What do most children like?

_____

d) How many children answered the questions?

_____

Read familiar words.

Topic 4 Progress check

1 Complete the words.

a)

10

t___n

b)

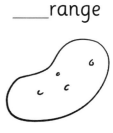

___range

c)

___ ___s

d)

___ean

e)

___ ___n

f)

___ineapple

2 Write sentences using these words.

a) three carrots There are.

_____

b) She mangoes likes.

_____

c) banana This is long yellow and

_____

d) you Do peas like?

_____

3 Circle the correct words.

lunch   breakfast   reading   eating

4 What do you like to eat? Draw a picture.
Write two sentences.

This is _____ .

I like _____ .

Topic 5 Let's have fun

Unit A Fun and games

1 Listen and tick ✓ the boxes.

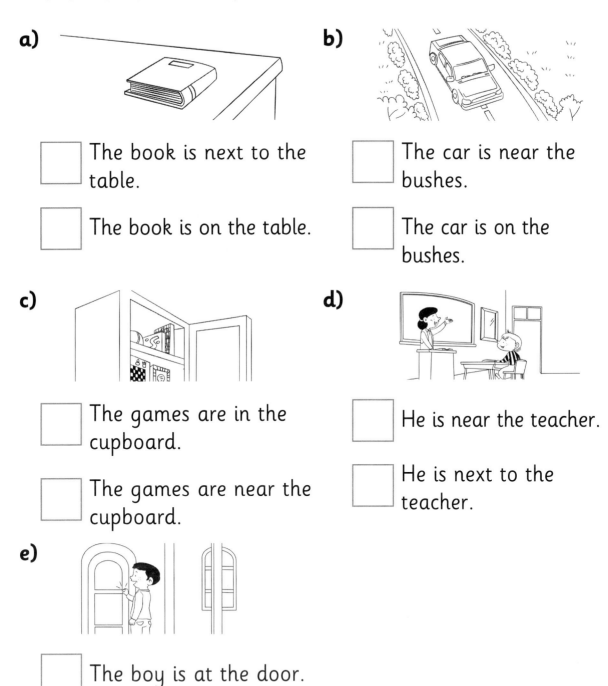

a)

☐ The book is next to the table.

☐ The book is on the table.

b)

☐ The car is near the bushes.

☐ The car is on the bushes.

c)

☐ The games are in the cupboard.

☐ The games are near the cupboard.

d)

☐ He is near the teacher.

☐ He is next to the teacher.

e)

☐ The boy is at the door.

☐ The boy is in the door.

2 **Where is the boy? Underline the correct words under each picture.**

a)

behind the table under the door

b)

in the cupboard on the cupboard

c)

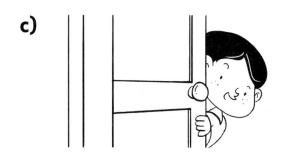

behind the door   on the door

d)

in the bed   under the bed

3 **Read the sentences. Draw the pictures.**

The girl is next to a sofa.

A boy is near a fridge.

4 Copy the sentences. Add capital letters and full stops.

a) she is on her bike

_____

_____

b) he is near the door

_____

_____

c) my sister plays with me

_____

_____

d) i like games

_____

_____

e) we play with a ball

_____

_____

5 **Read the words in the box. Find and circle the words in the sentences.**

> is   my   on   the   this   under   up   we

a) The cat is under the table.

b) The book is on the desk.

c) These are my socks.

d) This is my hat.

e) We are going up the tree.

6 **Write four new sentences. Use a word from the box in each sentence.**

a) _____

b) _____

c) _____

d) _____

7 Look at the snakes and ladders game.

- Write the numbers.
- Draw three snakes.
- Draw three ladders.
- Play the game in groups.

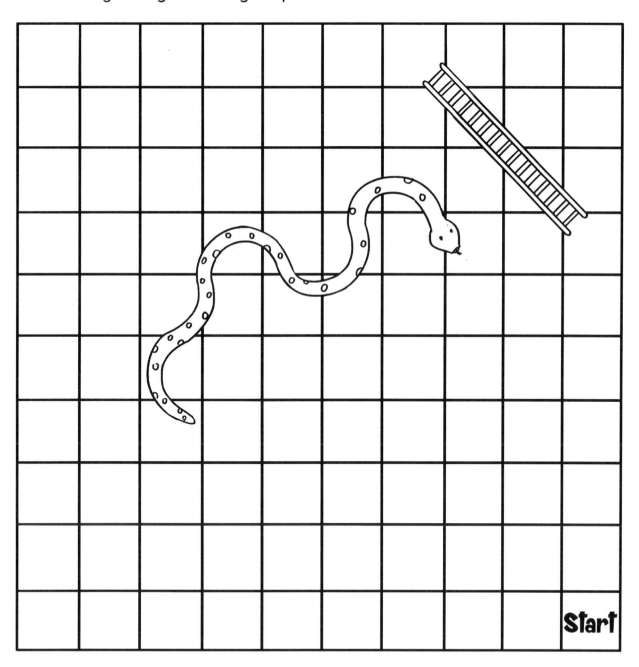

Unit B Sports

1 Match the words and the pictures. Write the words under the pictures.

athletics   netball   cycling   swimming   football
tennis   hockey   volleyball   judo   wrestling

a)

_____

b)

_____

c)

_____

d)

_____

e)

_____

f)

_____

g)

_____

h)

_____

i)

_____

j)

_____

Use common nouns.

2 Complete the picture.

- Draw the ball.
- Draw the goal.
- Draw a whistle.
- Colour in the T-shirts to show the two teams.

3 **Copy these sentences. Add capital letters and full stops.**

a) there are two teams

_____

_____

b) the referee has got a whistle

_____

_____

c) peter and ali like swimming in the sea

_____

_____

4 **Make sentences with these words. Add capital letters and full stops.**

a) i football play at the club

_____

_____

b) two goals there are on the field

_____

_____

c) likes cycling chris

_____

_____

5 Complete the sentences. Choose the best word.

a) The players are _____ the field. (on/in)

b) She plays tennis _____ the club. (up/at)

c) There _____ two nets on the football field. (is/are)

d) She _____ playing volleyball. (like/likes)

e) Let's _____ a computer game. (play/playing)

6 Draw a picture of a sport that you like playing. Write a sentence about it.

7 Look at the graph. Answer the questions.

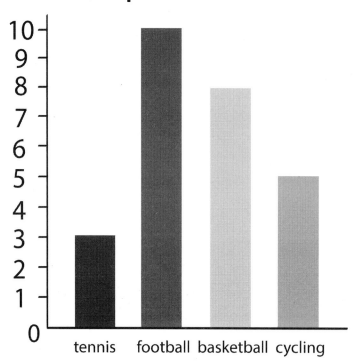

The sports that we like

a) How many children like playing tennis?

_____

b) How many children like cycling?

_____

c) What do most children like doing?

_____

d) How many children answered the questions?

_____

Unit C I am bored

1 What are they saying? Complete the speech bubbles.

Let's _____ football.

I'm _____ !

_____ _____ bored!

You _____ help _____.

2 Look at the pictures. Draw the hands on the clocks. Underline the correct words.

a)

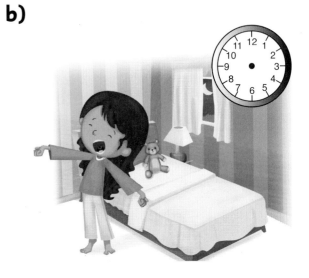

morning   afternoon

b)

morning   evening

c)

afternoon   night

d)

evening   morning

3 **Circle the correct words to complete the sentences.**

a) We go to school (at/on) seven o'clock.

b) My Mom makes supper (in/on) the evening.

c) My family have lunch together (at/on) Sundays.

d) We do not go to school (on/at) Saturdays.

e) I like running (at/in) the mornings.

f) My sister goes to bed (in/at) eight o'clock.

4 **Find the names of five days of the week in the puzzle. Write the words in the correct order.**

Topic 5 Progress check

1 Listen and tick ✓ the pictures that your teacher describes.

a)

b)

c)

2 Complete the sentences.

a)

He is _____ (at/on) the door.

b)

The book is next _____ (on/to) the chair.

c)

The cat is _____ (in/on) the lamp.

d)

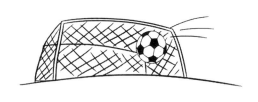

The ball is _____ (in/behind) the net.

3 Complete the words. Write the first letters.

a) _____ycling

b) _____ootball

c) _____ockey

d) _____udo

e) _____etball

f) _____olleyball

g) _____ _____estling

h) _____ _____imming

Topic 6 Out and about

Unit A What can I wear?

1 Tick ✓ the correct word to match the names of the clothes.

a) ☐ jacket
    ☐ jeans

b) ☐ skirt
    ☐ shorts

c) ☐ skirt
    ☐ scarf

d) ☐ sunglasses
    ☐ sandals

e) ☐ shorts
    ☐ T-shirt

f) ☐ glasses
    ☐ shoes

g) ☐ dress
    ☐ blouse

h) ☐ jumper
    ☐ trousers

i) ☐ gloves
    ☐ jacket

j) ☐ sock
    ☐ coat

Use singular and plural nouns.

2 **Look at the pictures and read the clues. Complete the words. The first one has been done for you.**

1	s	h	o	e	s
2					
3					
4					
5					

Clues

1  You wear two of these.

2  This word begins with *sk*.

3 Girls and boys wear these.

4 You can wear this when it is cold.

5 You wear these on your feet.

3 Listen to the story *Where Are My Jeans?*
Complete the sentences. Use words from
the box.

bed	dress	on	one	under

a) The jeans are _____ the bed.

b) The scarf is _____ the chair

c) The _____ is in the cupboard.

d) The T-shirt and jacket are on the _____.

e) There is _____ sock under the bed.

4 Draw these clothes on the washing line.

shorts   four socks   two T-shirts   a dress

Use singular and plural nouns and numbers.

5 Complete the words.

a)

_____ _____ ess

b)

_____ _____ oes

c)

_____ _____ asses

d)

_____ _____ irt

e)

_____ _____ ousers

f)

_____ _____ arf

6 These clothes words are jumbled. Write them correctly.

a) eansj _____

b) pmurje _____

c) tah _____

d) oscsk _____

7 Listen to the poems. Underline the words that rhyme.

1. Here are Grandpa's glasses
And here is Grandpa's hat
And here's the way he folds his arms
And takes a little nap.

2. One potato, two potatoes,
three potatoes, four!
Five potatoes, six potatoes,
Seven potatoes – and more!

3. I like paw-paws
And I like plums
I like painting
But I don't like drums.

4. Red, red, red,
    Touch your head.
Blue, blue, blue,
    Touch your shoe.
Black, black, black,
    Hands behind your back.
Green, green, green,
    Shout and scream!

Recognise and sound phonemes.

8 **Complete the sentences. Use words from the box.**

is   not   she   putting

a) This is my Grandma. _____ wears glasses.

b) That _____ my sister. She likes wearing dresses.

c) I do _____ like wearing a hat.

d) He is _____ on his clothes.

9 **Use these words to make sentences. Use capital letters and full stops.**

a) she her shoes taking off is

_____

b) I my socks putting on am

_____

c) likes he wearing shorts

_____

d) they wearing are gloves

_____

Unit B At the weekend

1 Read the poem and circle these words.

| a | and | ball | down | I'm | me | on | the | up |

The Ball Song

Throw   me   up   and   catch   me,
bounce   me   on   the   ground,
put   me   down   and   twist   me,
twizzle   me   around.

Drop   me   on   the   floor,
kick   me   at   the   wall.
Bounce   me!   Bounce   me!
I'm   a   bouncy   ball.

2 Underline the words in the poem that rhyme. Then write them here:

ground _____   wall _____

3 Find words in the poem that begin with the same letters.

b _____

tw _____

4 Draw lines to match the words that rhyme.

hat	lap
wall	three
me	play
day	cat
nap	ball

5 Fill in adjectives with the same beginning sound.

Example:

a **busy** bee

bouncy	busy	green	pretty

a) a _____ bee

b) _____ grass

c) a _____ ball

d) a _____ picture

6 **Read the story *Super Ben*. Then complete the sentences. Use words from the box.**

| plays | draws | feeds | splashes |

a) Ben _____ a picture.

b) He _____ the ducks.

c) He _____ on the roundabout.

d) He _____ in the puddles.

7 **Where does Ben go? Underline the correct answers.**

to the park   to school

on the roundabout   in the picture

8 **Read the sentence. Draw the picture.**

There are three brown ducks in a puddle.

9 Look at the pictures. Make sentences with words from the boxes.

Example: He cleans his bedroom on Saturdays.

play games
eat lunch together
clean his bedroom
have fun
play football
visit friends

at the weekend

on Saturdays

after school

_____

_____

_____

_____

_____

10 Write a sentence about what you do at the weekend.

_____

Unit C How I feel

1 Describe the weather. Choose a word from the box to complete each sentence.

> cloudy   rainy   sunny   windy

a)

It is a _____ day.

b)

It is a _____ day.

c)

It is a _____ day.

d)

It is a _____ day.

2 How does the weather make you feel?
Tick ✓ a box.

a) ☐ happy ☐ excited ☐ cross

b) ☐ happy ☐ excited ☐ cross

c) ☐ happy ☐ excited ☐ cross

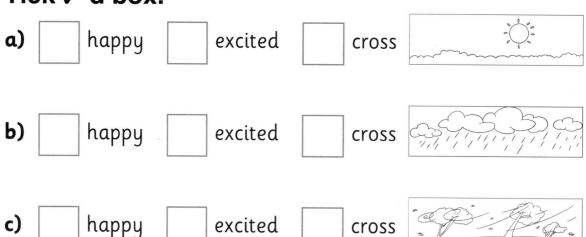

3 **Look at the pictures. Say the words. Which words have the same middle sounds as _pail_? Tick ✓ the pictures.**

a)

☐

b)

☐

c)

☐

d)

☐

4 **Complete these words with -_ay_.**

Mond ____ ____

Sund ____ ____

Thursd ____ ____

5 **Complete these words with -_ee_.**

tr ____ ____

f ____ ____ l

6 Read the sentences. Draw pictures to match.

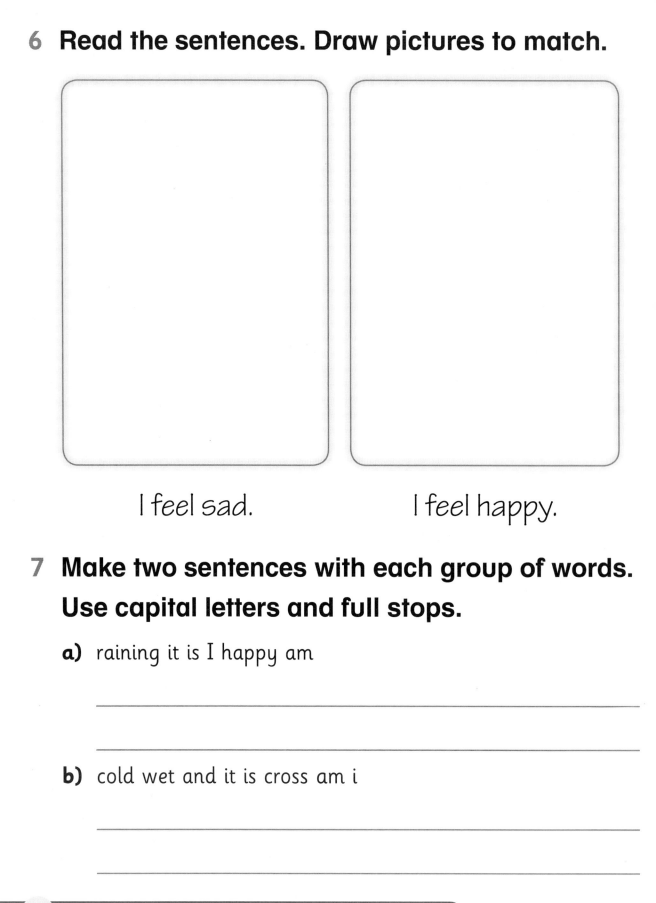

I feel sad.   I feel happy.

7 Make two sentences with each group of words. Use capital letters and full stops.

a) raining it is I happy am

_____

_____

b) cold wet and it is cross am i

_____

_____

Use adjectives; use capital letters and full stops.

8 Listen to the story *Bob's Secret Hideaway*.
Make sentences about each picture. Use the
words under the pictures.

a)

friends his and Bob are
the treehouse in

_____

_____

_____

_____

b)

feels Bob lonely sad and

_____

_____

_____

_____

9 Match the words that rhyme.

know   saw

noise   had

sad   toys

door   back

crack   glow

10 Work in groups to play *The Weather Game*.

- Take turns.
- Spin a spinner.
- Read the instructions.
- Play the game.

8	9	10	FINISH
		Go back to NINE.	
7	**6**	**5**	**4**
Go on to EIGHT		Go back to TWO.	Go on to SIX.
START	**1**	**2**	**3**
	Go on to TWO.		Miss a turn.

Topic 6 Progress check

1 Write the correct word under each picture.

boots	glasses	sandals	shorts	sweatshirt
	coat	jeans	T-shirt	sock

_____ _____ _____

_____ _____ _____

_____ _____ _____

2 **Make sentences with each group of words. Use capital letters and full stops.**

a) sunny it is

_____

b) cross am i

_____

c) we games play Saturdays on

_____

3 **Complete the sentences using a word from the box.**

| play | draws | feeds | splash |

a) I _____ in the puddles.

b) He _____ the ducks.

c) They _____ on the roundabout.

d) She _____ pictures.

Topic 7 Our world

Unit A Homes

1 **Label the outside parts of the house. Use the words in the box. Find the words in the Student's Book on page 44.**

door	garage	garden	gate	roof	window

2 **Label the furniture in the kitchen. Use the words in the box.**

chair   cooker   cupboard   fridge   sink

table   tap   washing machine

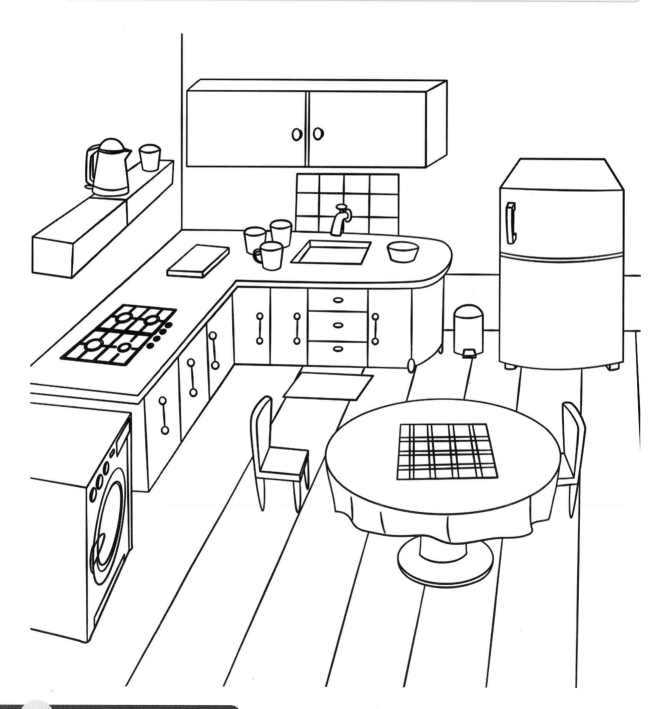

Use common nouns.

3 **Look at the pictures. Complete each sentence with the best word from the box.**

| wheels | quiet | water | noisy |

This home is _____.   This home is on _____.

4 **Read the sentences. Draw a picture for each sentence.**

This home is big.   This home is for a bird!

5 Listen to the story. Tick ✓ the sentence that matches each picture.

a)

☐ This is my new home.

☐ This is our new boat.

b)

☐ My new bed is big!

☐ My new home is noisy.

c)

☐ I am happy.

☐ I am sad.

d)

☐ I haven't got a friend. I am sad.

☐ This is my new friend. I am happy.

6 **Look at the first letter of these words.**
Write them in alphabetical order.

a) garage   door   roof

_____

b) tap   sink   fridge

_____

7 **Find these words in the word puzzle:**

a) One thing from a bedroom _____

_____

b) Two things from a bathroom _____

_____

c) Three things from a kitchen _____

_____

a	c	o	o	k	e	r	f
s	h	o	w	e	r	y	r
c	t	m	q	t	r	n	i
a	c	b	a	t	h	v	d
m	u	e	l	l	x	w	g
i	o	d	r	e	c	t	e

8 Complete the sentences.

Some homes are _____ up.

Some _____ are noisy.

Some homes _____ quiet.

Some homes float on _____.

Some homes _____ wheels.

9 Draw a picture of your own home. Write a sentence to describe it. Use some of the words in the box.

big high home my nice noisy quiet small warm

_____

_____

Use adjectives.

10 Listen to the instructions. Draw the house.

- Draw a rectangle.

- Draw a triangle on top of the house rectangle. This is the roof.

- Draw one door and three windows.

- Colour in the house.

11 Listen to the story *A New Home* again.

12 Copy the sentences in the correct order.

I like playing football with Jo.

We are moving to a new home.

One day I make a new friend, Jo.

My new home is small but it has a big garden.

_____

_____

_____

_____

_____

_____

_____

13 Tell the story to your partner.

Recognise familiar words.

Unit B Plants and animals

1 Draw a picture of a plant. Colour in your picture. Label the following parts:

leaf	roots	stem

2 Choose the correct word and complete the sentences.

a) Plants grow from _____. (seeds/goats)

b) Plants need soil, _____ and water to grow. (sun/fun)

3 **Listen to the story _The Very Big Carrot_. Who helps to pull up the carrot? Label the pictures.**

| Mrs Brown | Mr Brown | boy | girl | cat | goat | horse |

a)

_____

b)

_____

c)

_____

d)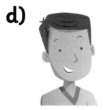

_____

e)

_____

f)

_____

g)

_____

4 **Read the story of *Jack and the Beanstalk*. Circle these words in the story:**

| an | and | are | his | is | the | they |

Jack and his mother are poor. They have to sell their cow.

Jack gives the cow to an old man.

Jack gets some beans.

Jack's mother is cross.

The beans grow.

Jack meets the giant.

Jack finds gold.

Jack's mother is happy.

5 **Answer the questions. Circle the correct answer.**

a) What does Jack sell? cow giant

b) What does Jack get? beans flowers

c) What do the beans do? grow plant

d) What does Jack find? gold green

6 Read these sentences from the story *The Very Big Carrot.*

The goat helps.

The girl helps.

The cat helps.

Mrs Brown pulls up the carrots.

The horse helps.

They all fall over!

Mr Brown helps.

The boy helps.

7 Listen to the story. Copy the sentences in the correct order.

Recognise and copy familiar words.

8 Look at the diagram. Listen to the text.

The life cycle of a bean plant

9 Copy the correct sentence under each picture.

There are seeds inside the pod.

We plant the seed in the ground.

The seed grows.

The plant has flowers.

There are beans on the plant.

Unit C Living in our world

1 **Read the story *The Oak Tree* in the Student's Book. Find words in the story to label this picture of an oak tree.**

a)

_____

b)

_____

c)

_____

d)

_____

e) _____

2 **Find the names of these animals in the story.**

a)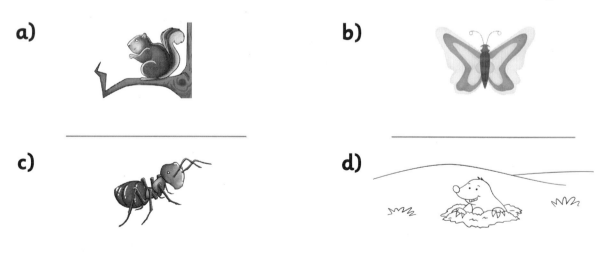

b)

c)

d)

_____

3 Write the correct words under the photographs.

a)

_____

b)

_____

c)

_____

d)

_____

desert   mountains   jungle   South Pole

4 Complete the sentences with words from the box.

dry   hot   wet   cold

a) It is _____ at the South Pole.

b) A desert is _____ .

c) It is _____ and _____ in a jungle.

5 Label the things in the picture with words from the box.

butterfly	crow	bat	wasp	mole
squirrel	owl	caterpillar	ant	worm
fox	beetle	woodpecker	rabbit	

a) _____

b) _____

c) _____

d) _____

e) _____

f) _____

g) _____

h) _____

i) _____

j) _____

k) _____

l) _____

m) _____

n) _____

Recognise and copy familiar words.

6 Draw a picture of one of these places:

- a jungle
- a mountain
- a very cold place
- a very hot place

7 Complete the sentences about your picture.

This is a _____.

It is _____ and

_____.

_____ live in the

_____.

8 **Read the story *The Oak Tree* again. Complete the sentences using the words in the box.**

the	are	has	in	is	and

a) A tree _____ branches _____ a trunk.

b) There _____ bark on _____ trunk.

c) Crows and bats live _____ the branches.

d) These _____ the roots of the tree.

9 **Find words in the story that rhyme with these words.**

a) box _____

b) grow _____

c) cat _____

d) hole _____

Recognise familiar words; sound phonemes.

10 **Look at the map. Label the map with these names.**

Africa	North America
Asia	South America
Europe	Australia

Our world

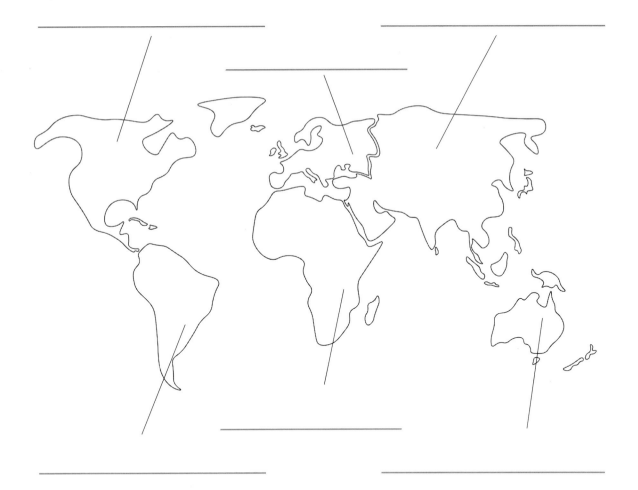

Topic 7 Progress check

1 Listen and underline the word that you hear.

a) door floor

b) gate Kate

c) fridge dish

d) bin pin

e) Tuesday Thursday

f) wheel meal

2 Circle the word that matches the picture.

a)

leaf   branch

b)

mouse   squirrel

c)

jungle   desert

d)

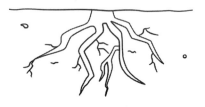

bark   roots

3 Complete the sentences. Use words from the box.

and   are   cold   in   is   two

a) There _____ lots of leaves on the tree.

b) My house has _____ bedrooms.

c) The kettle _____ in the kitchen.

d) It is very hot _____ dry in the desert.

e) The seeds grow _____ the bean pod.

f) The South Pole is _____.

Topic 8 Healthy bodies

Unit A My body

1 **Use the words in the box to label the picture.**

| arm | foot | hand | head | leg | neck | tummy |

2 **The names of parts of the body are in the box.**
Find the words in the word search.

arm	back	eyes	hand	head
leg	neck	nose	shoulder	toes

g	t	t	k	s	d	h	a
s	h	o	u	l	d	e	r
m	a	e	q	e	b	a	m
p	n	s	e	g	a	d	h
q	d	w	y	f	c	v	g
z	e	n	e	c	k	j	z
x	n	o	s	e	v	c	x
y	l	m	n	o.	p	q	r

3 Complete the sentences. Use words from the box.

head   body   leg   back

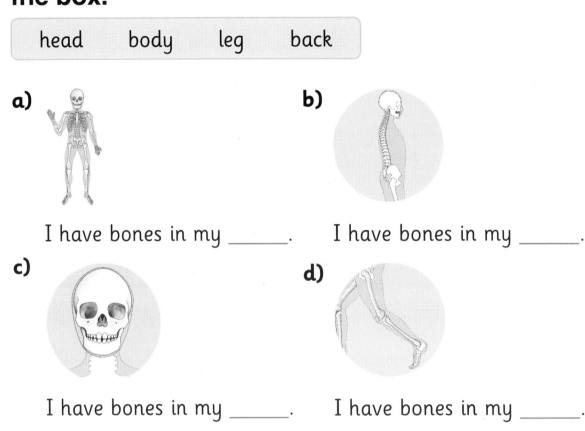

a)

I have bones in my _____.

b)

I have bones in my _____.

c)

I have bones in my _____.

d)

I have bones in my _____.

4 Draw a picture of your arm. Where are the bones? Label your picture.

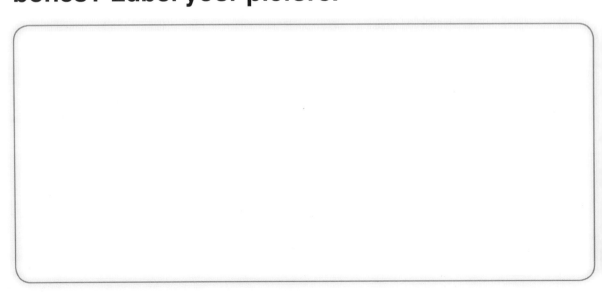

Recognise and copy familiar words.

5 Make words. Add *-ing*.

a) paint ____ ____ ____

b) press ____ ____ ____

c) eat ____ ____ ____

d) wash ____ ____ ____

6 Look at the words on the board. Draw a picture about one of the words.

7 **Draw lines to match the parts of the body and the senses.**

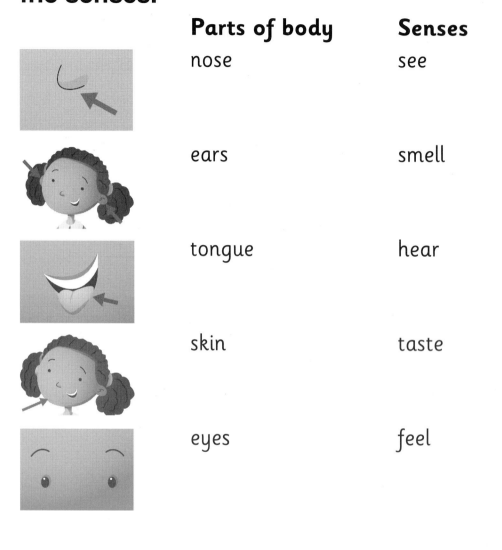

Parts of body	Senses
nose	see
ears	smell
tongue	hear
skin	taste
eyes	feel

8 Complete the sentences.

a) I see with my _____ .

b) I taste with _____ _____ .

c) I feel _____ _____ _____ .

d) I _____ with my ears.

e) I _____ _____ _____ nose.

9 **Where do you have bones? Complete the list.**

You have bones in your _____ , your _____ ,

your _____ , your _____ , your _____

and your _____ .

10 **Draw a picture of your hands. Label your hands. Use these words:**

| left hand right hand finger bone nail |

11 Draw pictures. Label your pictures.

Things I can hear	Things I can see
Things I can taste	**Things I can smell**

Give personal information.

12 Complete these poems about your senses.
Give your poems titles.

[title] _____

I use my hands

for _____

and for _____

and for _____.

I use my hands all the time!

[title] _____

I hear with my _____

And I _____ with my

_____.

I _____ with

my _____

And I _____ with my

_____.

Unit B Healthy and sick

1 **Read again about washing your hands on page 54 of the Student's Book. Complete the instructions.**

1. Wet your _____.

2. Put _____ on your hands.

3. _____ your hands together.

4. _____ to 20!

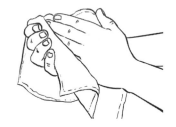

5. _____ off the soap.

6. _____ your hands on a clean cloth.

Use imperatives.

2 Join the words to make sentences.

Put water and soap   your nails.

Then rub   the soap off your hands.

Scrub   to 20!

Count   your hands.

Rinse   on your hands.

Dry   your hands together.

3 Write the sentences here.

_____

_____

_____

_____

_____

4 Complete the instructions. Use words and sentences from the box.

> toothbrush
>
> toothpaste
>
> a cup of water
>
> Rinse your mouth.
>
> Wet the toothbrush.
>
> Brush your teeth.
>
> Rinse your toothbrush.
>
> Put toothpaste on the toothbrush.

How to brush your teeth

You will need:

toothbrush

_____

_____

What you do:

1. _____

2. _____

3. _____

4. _____

5. _____

5 **Match the sentences and the pictures.**

Write the sentences in the speech bubbles.

Wash your feet.	Wet the soil.
Pick up the book.	Wash your hands.

a)

b)

c)

d)

6 Think about how many glasses of water you drink every day.

- Write your estimate here: _____ glasses

7 Keep a record for one week. Keep a tally here.

Days	Monday	Tuesday	Wednesday	Thursday	Friday
Number of glasses of water					
Total					

8 Complete the sentences.

I drank _____ glasses of water every day.

I drank _____ glasses of water this week.

Unit C Oh no! I am sick!

1 Look at the pictures. Write the illness under the correct picture.

> I am going to be sick.
>
> I have got a headache.
>
> I have got a tummy ache.
>
> I have got a sore throat.
>
> I have got a cold.
>
> I have got earache.

a) _____

b) _____

c) _____

d) _____

e) _____

f) _____

2 Match the answers to the questions.

a) Do you feel sick?   No, I am not.

b) Is your head sore?   Yes, she does.

c) Are you well?   Yes, it is.

d) Does she have a cold?   Yes, they are.

e) Is he well?   Yes, I do.

f) Are they sick?   No, he isn't.

3 Complete the conversation.

Sam: Do _____ feel sick?

Anna: Yes, _____ do.

Sam: _____ your head sore?

Anna: No, it _____ not.

Sam: _____ you have a cold?

Anna: _____, I do.

Sam: Get better soon!

4 **Read the story *In the Hospital* on page 55 of the Student's Book. Complete the sentences with words from the box.**

| a | has | in | is |

a) Raj is _____ hospital.

b) The children make _____ card for Raj.

c) Raj _____ a sore leg.

d) He _____ feeling better.

5 **Make a card for Raj. Write a message and draw some pictures.**

Dear Raj
Get well soon.
From,
Abdul

6 **Listen to the story *Sam the Big, Bad Cat* again. Complete the sentences.**

a)

_____ doesn't feel well.

b)

Sam is _____ the table.

c)

Sam is _____ the cupboard.

d)

Sam is _____ the shower.

e)

Tom doesn't _____ well.

f)

_____ feels better.

Use present simple verbs and prepositions.

7 **Make sentences about the story with these words. Use capital letters and full stops.**

a) Tom has cat bad big a

_____

b) Sam not does well feel

_____

c) to the vet Let's go

_____

d) Sam in the cupboard hides

_____

e) in the shower Sam hides

_____

f) Tom Sam finds

_____

g) Tom not does well feel

_____

Topic 8 Progress check

1 Listen and number the parts of the body.

2 What do you need? Choose and write two words.

a) I need _____ and _____ to wash my hands.

soap   toothpaste   water

b) I need _____ and _____ to brush my teeth.

soap   toothpaste   water

3 What is the first letter of each word? Circle the letter.

a)

h   t

b)

d   b

4 Make sentences. Use capital letters and full stops.

a) I well don't feel

_____

b) he sick is

_____

Unit A My town

1   **Write the names of the places. Choose words
from the box or add your own labels.**

dentist	doctor	library	park	school
shoe shop	supermarket	swimming pool		

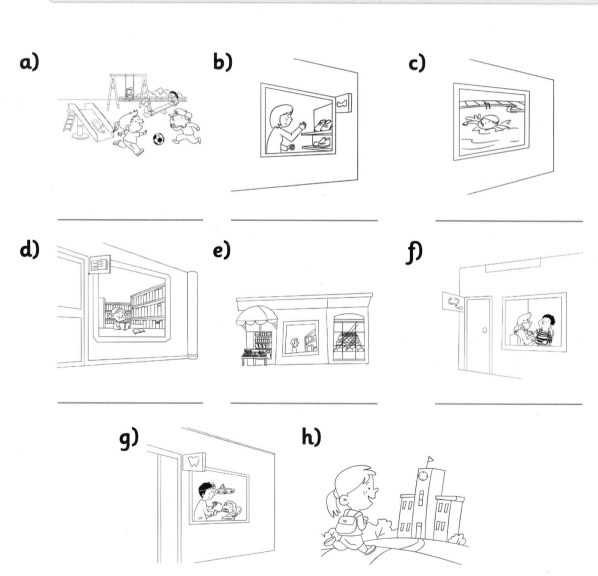

a)

b)

c)

d)

e)

f)

g)

h)

2 Draw a picture of a place you like to visit.

3 Write two sentences about your picture.

Start like this:

This is _____

_____ .

I like to _____

_____ .

4 Listen to the story *A Day Out* again.

- Follow on the map.
- Trace the road in colour.

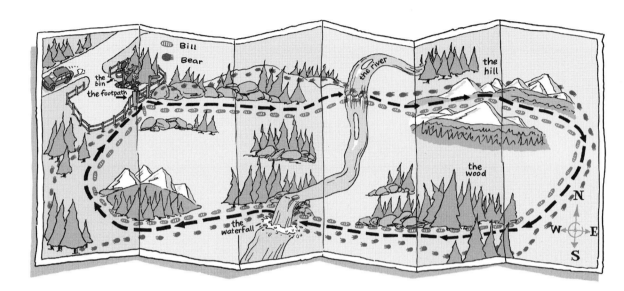

- Where do Bill and the bear go?
- Write the names of the places on the map here:

the footpath

5 Draw lines to match the words and the pictures.

a)

river

b)

hill

c)

wood

d)

waterfall

e)

litter bin

6 Choose the correct word to complete the sentences.

a) Bill went _____ a walk. (for/to)

b) He went _____ the hill. (up/into)

c) He went _____ a river. (over/behind)

7 Imagine that you go out for the day.

Where do you go?

- Draw a map.
- Label the places on your map.
- Look in the box for some ideas!

pool   mountain   river   sea   dam   park   museum   beach

Unit B A day out

1 Match the words and the pictures.

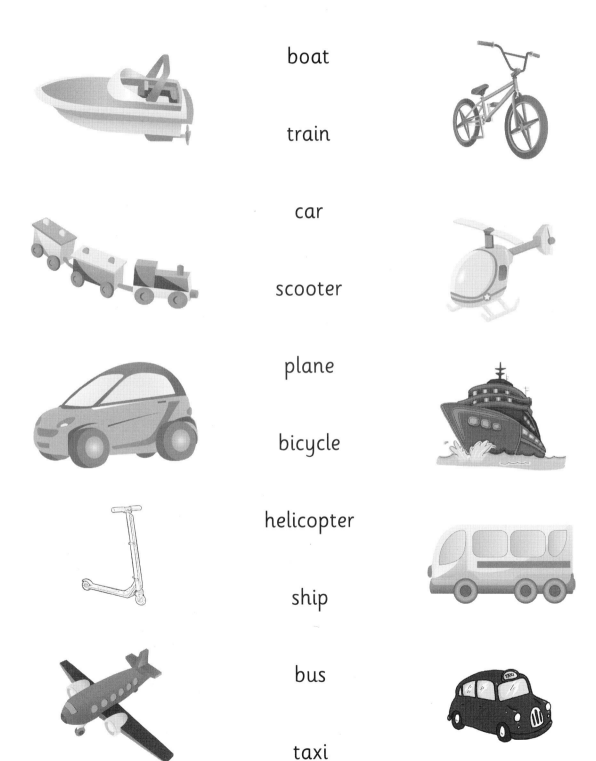

boat

train

car

scooter

plane

bicycle

helicopter

ship

bus

taxi

2 Colour in the pictures.

- The plane is red.
- The boat is green and blue.
- The taxi is red and black.

3 Complete the pictures.

- The bike has two wheels.
- The bus has six wheels.

 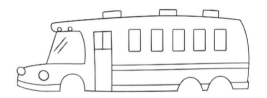

4 Draw a picture of a small boat and a big ship.

5 Complete the chart.

One	More than one
train	trains
car	
taxi	
plane	
scooter	
bike	

6 Underline the correct words.

a) There (is/are) two cars in the park.

b) The taxi (is/are) next to the bus.

c) There are four (scooter/scooters) on the road.

d) Where is the (train/trains)?

7 Read the story *At the Bus Station* again.

Tick ✓ the sentence that matches each picture.

a) ☐ They are packing suitcases.

☐ They are at the station.

b) ☐ They are playing at the station.

☐ They are at the station.

c) ☐ The girl is not there.

☐ The girl is there.

d) ☐ The girl is talking to a friend.

☐ The girl is packing a suitcase.

8 **Find these words in the sentences.**
Circle the words.

are   don't   here   is   our   she   the   there   to   very   we

a) We   are   going   to   visit   our   cousins.

b) The   train   station   is   very   busy.

c) I   don't   know.   She   was   here.

d) Is   she   here?

e) There   you   are!

9 **Make questions with these words.**
Use a capital letter to start each question.

a) he here is ?

_____

b) she is where ?

_____

c) you like trains do ?

_____

d) he does have a bike ?

_____

10 Look at the graph. Answer the questions.

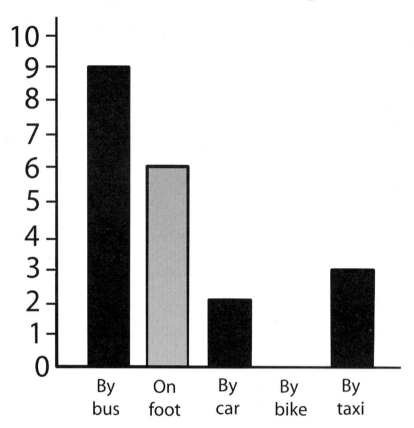

a) How many learners come by bus?

_____

b) How many learners walk?

_____

c) How do most learners get to school?

_____

d) Which type of transport do no learners use?

_____

Use interrogatives; use numbers to count.

Unit C Holidays

1 Read the story *Around the World* on pages 62–63 of the Student's Book again. Find the places on this map.

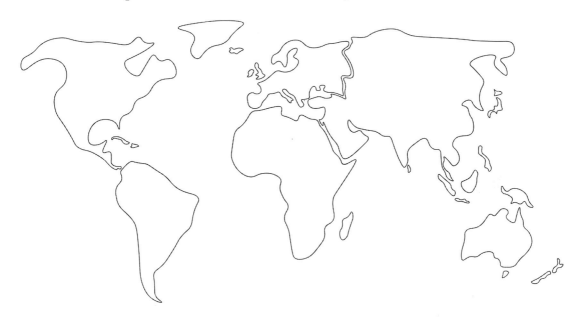

2 Colour in these places in yellow on the map.

- South America
- Africa
- India
- China

3 Colour the other places in green. Colour the sea blue.

4 Draw a picture of something you think you can see in each place.

5 Make sentences with words from each column.

  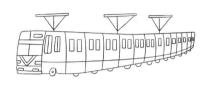

Let's go   on the train.

I like playing   you going?

We are   with my cousins.

She is going   they doing?

Where are   painting the house.

What are   to the park.

Write the sentences here.

a) _____

b) _____

c) _____

d) _____

e) _____

f) _____

Recognise and copy familiar words.

6 Read the story *Around the World* on pages 62–63 of the Student's Book again.

7 Underline three words to answer each question.

    a) Which countries do they visit?

       India   China   Africa   America

    b) How do they travel?

       train   bike   plane   boat

    c) What do they see?

       bats   animals   houses   boats

8 Find words in the story that rhyme with:

a) train _____

b) snow _____

9 **Read the clues. Complete the puzzle. Most of the words are in the story _Around the World_.**

Clues

1. The place where you live. My h ____ ____ ____

2. A place where we all live. w ____ ____ ____ ____

3. This flies up in the sky. p ____ ____ ____ ____

4. A big country. C ____ ____ ____ ____

5. Where _____ we go? d ____ ____

6. This stops at a station. t ____ ____ ____ ____

7. This word means talk or speak. s ____ ____

8. This is yellow and round and up in the sky. s ____ ____

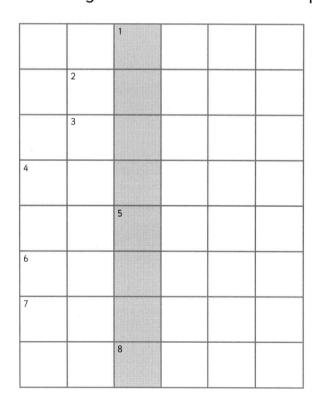

What new word can you see down the middle?

_____

The alphabet

Trace the letters. Draw a picture of something beginning with this letter.

Aa

Bb

Cc

Dd

Ee

Ff

Gg

Hh

Ii

Jj

Kk

Ll

Mm

Nn

Oo

Pp

Form higher and lower case letters.

Qq

Rr

Ss

Tt

Uu

Vv

Ww

Xx

Yy

Zz

Numbers

Trace the numbers and number words.

• 1 1 1 1

one   one   one

•• 2 2 2 2

two   two   two

••• 3 3 3 3

three   three   three

•••• 4 4 4 4

four   four   four

••••• 5 5 5 5

five   five   five

Copy number names.

6 6 6 6
six   six   six

7 7 7 7
seven   seven   seven

8 8 8 8
eight   eight   eight

9 9 9 9
nine   nine   nine

10 10 10 10
ten   ten   ten

Shapes

Trace the names.

star

rectangle

triangle

heart

circle

square

Copy nouns (shapes).